The Rhymers' Club

In 1890 W B Yeats and Ernest Rhys founded a poetry club. Based mainly at Fleet Street's immortal 'Ye Olde Cheshire Cheese' pub with occasional appearances at the Domino room in the Café Royal poets gathered together to dine and drink.

Whilst it was based on a core of poets many others attended on an ad hoc basis including Oscar Wilde, Francis Thompson & Lord Alfred Douglas. The camaraderie, banter and poetry that played out in their dreams, ambitions and for many, their difficult lives led Yeats to call them 'the tragic generation'.

As well as their enthusiastic social forays they printed two anthologies of verse. The first in 1892 and the second in 1894. For all the talent it could call upon the print runs were only in their hundreds.

Part of a poet's obligation is to move the boundaries of society, to write what others shun. And whilst that is certainly the case with our group in terms of writing in one glaring respect they were very Victorian. The members of the club were only men.

Arthur Ransome sums up their existence as "... the Rhymer's Club used to meet, to drink from tankards, smoke clay pipes, and recite their own poetry".

Whilst their initial aims were food, drink, camaraderie and bragging, the reality is that their poetry gives us so much more.

THE RHYMERS CLUB MEMBERS
ERNEST DOWSON
EDWIN J ELLIS
G A GREENE
LIONEL JOHNSON
RICHARD LE GALLIENNE
VICTOR PLARR
ERNEST RADFORD
ERNEST RHYS
T W ROLLESTON
ARTHUR SYMONS
JOHN TODHUNTER
W B YEATS

Index of Contents

Love and Death (Æsop's Fable) by Ernest Radford
Epitaphium Citharistriæ by Victor Plarr
Beatrice's Song (From 'The Poison Flower') by John Todhunter
The Pathfinder by G A Greene
The Broken Tryst by Arthur Symons
New Words and Old by Edwin J Ellis
A Ring's Secret by T W Rolleston
The Wedding of Pale Bronwen by Ernest Rhys
Beauty Accurst by Richard Le Gallienne
O Mors! quam amara est memoria tua homini pacem habenti in substantiis suis! by Ernest Dowson.
The Sonnet by G A Greene
A Burden of Easter Vigil by Lionel Johnson
To One Beloved by John Todhunter
Music and Memory by Arthur Symons
In a Norman Church by Victor Plarr
Father Gilligan by W B Yeats
Amor Umbratilis by Ernest Dowson
At the Hearth by Edwin J Ellis
Keats' Grave by G A Greene
On Marlowe by Ernest Rhys
At Citoyenne Tussaud's by Victor Plarr
Ballade of the 'Cheshire Cheese' by T W Rolleston
The Last Music by Lionel Johnson
A Death in the Forest by Arthur Symons
'Onli Deathe' by Ernest Radford
Ad Domnulam Suam by Ernest Dowson
Dedication of 'Irish Tales' by W B Yeats
Quatrain (The Epitaph on Hafiz, a Young Linnet) by Ernest Rhys
Javanese Dancers: A Silhouette by Arthur Symons
Chorus from 'Iphigeneia in Aulis' by John Todhunter
To a Greek Gem by Victor Plarr
Arts Lough by G A Greene
In Falmouth Harbour by Lionel Johnson
A Choice of Likenesses by Ernest Radford
To Autumn by Richard Le Gallienne
Vanitas by Ernest Dowson
A Fairy Song by W B Yeats
Mothers of Men by Edwin J Ellis
Chatterton in Holborn by Ernest Rhys
To a Passionist by Lionel Johnson
Freedom in a Suburb by Ernest Radford
Quatrain: Les Bourgeoises by Ernest Rhys
Drifting by G A Greene
Villanelle of Sunset by Ernest Dowson
The Lake Isle of Innisfree by W B Yeats
A Sundial: Flowers of Time by Ernest Radford
Twilight-Piece by Victor Plarr
Sunset in the City by Richard Le Gallienne

AT THE RHYMERS' CLUB

THE TOAST

By Ernest Rhys

Set fools unto their folly!
Our folly is pure wit,
As "twere the Muse turned folly:
For poets' melancholy, —
We will not think of it.

As once Rare Ben and Herrick
Set older Fleet Street mad,
With wit not esoteric,
And laughter that was lyric,
And roystering rhymes and glad:

As they, we drink defiance
To-night to all but Rhyme,
And most of all to Science,
And all such skins of lions
Thai hide the ass of time.

To-night, to rhyme as they did
Were well, —ah, were it ours,
Who find the Muse degraded,
And changed, I fear, and faded,
Her laurel crown and flowers.

Ah rhymers, for that sorrow
The more overtakes delight,
The more this madness borrow: —
If care be hug to-morrow,
To toast Queen Rhyme to-night.

WHAT OF THE DARKNESS?

(To the Happy Dead People)

By Richard Le Gallienne

What of the Darkness? Is it very fair?
Are there great calms and find ye silence there?
Like soft-shut lilies all your faces glow
With some strange peace our faces never know,
With some great faith our faces never dare.
Dwells it in Darkness? Do ye find it there?

Is it a Bosom where tired heads may lie?
Is it a Mouth to kiss our weeping dry?
Is it a Hand to still the pulse's leap?
Is it a Voice that holds the runes of sleep?
Day shows us not such comfort anywhere.
Dwells it in Darkness? Do ye find it there?

Out of the day's deceiving light we call,
Day that shows man so great and God so small,
That hides the stars and magnifies the grass;
O! is the Darkness too a lying glass,
Or undistracted do ye find Truth there? —
What of the Darkness? Is it very fair?

BY THE STATUE OF KING CHARLES THE FIRST AT CHARING CROSS

By Lionel Johnson

Sombre and rich, the skies;
Great glooms, and starry plains.
Gently the night wind sighs;
Else a vast silence reigns.

The splendid silence clings
Around me: and around
The saddest of all kings
Crowned, and again discrowned.

Comely and calm, he rides
Hard by his own Whitehall:
Only the night wind glides:
No crowds, nor rebels, brawl.

Gone, too, his Court: and yet.
The stars his courtiers are:

Stars in their stations set;
And every wandering star.

Alone he rides, alone,
The fair and fatal king:
Dark night is all his own,
That strange and solemn thing.

Which are more full of fate:
The stars: or those sad eyes?
Which are more still and great:
Those brows: or the dark skies?

Although his whole heart yearn
In passionate tragedy:
Never was face so stern
With sweet austerity.

Vanquished in life, his death
By beauty made amends:
The passing of his breath
Won his defeated ends.

Brief life, and hapless? Nay:
Through death, life grew sublime.
Speak after sentence? Yea:
And to the end of time.

Armoured he rides, his head
Bare to the stars of doom:
He triumphs now, the dead.
Beholding London's gloom.

Our wearier spirit faints,
Vexed in the world's employ:
His soul was of the Saints;
And art to him was joy.

King, tried in fires of woe!
Men hunger for thy grace:
And through the night I go,
Loving thy mournful face.

Yet, when the city sleeps;
When all the cries are still:
The stars and heavenly deeps
Work out their perfect will.

A MAN WHO DREAMED OF FAIRYLAND

By W B Yeats

I

He stood among a crowd at Drumahair,
His heart hung all upon a silken dress,
And he had known at last some tenderness
Before earth made of him her sleepy care;
But when a man poured fish into a pile,
It seemed they raised their little silver heads
And sang how day a Druid twilight sheds
Upon a dim, green, well-beloved isle.
Where people love beside star-laden seas;
How Time may never mar their fairy vows
Under the woven roofs of quicken boughs; —
The singing shook him out of his new ease.

II

As he went by the sands of Lisadill
His mind ran all on money cares and fears,
And he had known at last some prudent years
Before they heaped his grave under the hill;
But while he passed before a plashy place,
A lug-worm with its gray and muddy mouth
Sang how somewhere to north or east or south
There dwelt a gay, exulting, gentle race;
And how beneath those three times blessed skies
A Danaan fruitage makes a shower of moons
And as it falls awakens leafy tunes; —
And at that singing he was no more wise.

III

He mused beside the well of Scanavin,
He mused upon his mockers. Without fail
His sudden vengeance were a country tale
Now that deep earth has drunk his body in;
But one small knot-grass growing by the rim
Told where — ah, little, all-unneeded voice! —
Old Silence bids a lonely folk rejoice.
And chaplet their calm brows with leafage dim

And how, when fades the sea-strewn rose of day,
A gentle feeling wraps them like a fleece.
And all their trouble dies into its peace; —
The tale drove his fine angry mood away.

IV

He slept under the hill of Lugnagall,
And might have known at last unhaunted sleep
Under that cold and vapour-turbaned steep,
Now that old earth had taken man and all:
Were not the worms that spired about his bones
A-telling with their low and reedy cry
Of how God leans His hands out of the sky,
To bless that isle with honey in His tones.
That none may feel the power of squall and wave,
And no one any leaf-crowned dances miss
Until He burn up Nature with a kiss; —
The man has found no comfort in the grave.

CARMELITE NUNS OF THE PERPETUAL ADORATION

By Ernest Dowson

Calm, sad, secure; behind high convent walls;
These watch the sacred lamp, these watch and pray:
And it is one with them, when evening falls;
And one with them, the cold return of day.

These heed not time: their nights and days they make
Into a long, returning rosary;
Whereon their lives are threaded for Christ's sake:
Meekness and vigilance and chastity.

A vowed patrol, in silent companies,
Life long they keep before the living Christ:
In the dim church, their prayers and penances.
Are fragrant incense to the Sacrificed.

Outside, the world is wild and passionate;
Man's weary laughter, and his sick despair
Entreat at their impenetrable gate:
They heed no voices in their dream of prayer.

They saw the glory of the world displayed,

They saw the bitter of it, and the sweet:
They knew the roses of the world should fade,
And be trod under by the hurrying feet.

Therefore they rather put away desire,
And crossed their hands and came to Sanctuary;
And veiled their heads and put on coarse attire:
Because their comeliness was vanity.

And there they rest; they have serene insight
Of the illuminating dawn to be:
Mary's sweet Star dispels for them the night,
The proper darkness of humanity.

Calm, sad, serene; with faces worn and mild:
Surely their choice of vigil is the best?
Yea! for our roses fade, the world is wild;
But there, beside the altar, there, is rest.

LOVE AND DEATH

(Æsop's Fable)

By Ernest Radford

Love, on a summer day,
Faint with heat,
Tired with play,
Came to a grotto fair,
And courted slumber there,
And flung his darts away.

This was, the Fable saith,
The very cave of Death;
But this Love did not know:
As he had sped a shaft
With more than common craft,
Once — in his sleep — he laughed:
At dawn he rose to go.

Love was at parting fain
To have his darts again: —
'O Love, beware, beware!
The shafts of Death are there,
Of mortal man the bane!'
But Love cared not a stiver:

Intent on human hearts
He gathered to his quiver
His own with Death's black darts;
And glorious in the morning
He winged his golden way,
Sweet maidens had forewarning
That Love was on the way,
Strong men all labour scorning,
Did nothing on that day,
For dallying with a maiden
Is neither work nor play.

Old men and women saddened
In the dragging of the years,
On a sudden gladdened
To laughter and to tears.
Love was on earth again,
Intending ill to none.
(He wotted not of pain
Blind creature of the Sun!)
He knew not what he did,
Nor rested till 'twas done.
But old and young
He rushed amid.
And shot his arrows
Everyone.

And some cried out — 'Ah, Death he deals!'
And surely Death did come,
And others cried — ''tis Love, 'tis Love!'
And Love there was for some.

EPITAPHIUM CITHARISTRAE

By Victor Plarr

Stand not uttering sedately
Trite oblivious praise above her!
Rather say you saw her lately
Lightly kissing her last lover.

Whisper not, 'There is a reason
Why we bring her no white blossom.'
Since the snowy bloom's in season
Strow it on her sleeping bosom!

Oh, for it would be a pity
To o'erpraise her or to flout her.
She was wild, and sweet, and witty —
Let's not say dull things about her.

BEATRICE'S SONG

From ' The Poison Flower'

By John Todhunter

A chamber with a window overlooking RAPACCINI'S garden.

GUASCONTI alone. BEATRICE sings in the garden.

SONG

Heap me a mound of holy spice.
With camphor, sandal, cinnamon,
Gums and rich balms, like that whereon
The magican phœnix burns and dies!
There let pale women hush their cries
To do in desolate array
Soft rites, and chant low litanies,
Till thunders roll around the skirts of day:
Then fling the torch and come away.,
Come away, and leave the kindled pyre
Where Love lies dead, that was the world's desire!

[**GUASCONTI** listens intently, then runs to the window, looks out and draws back disappointed.

GUASCONTI
Earth has her siren: all my senses sing,
And the lone caverns of my inward ear
Sound on, like musing shells that lull themselves
To sad content, with ocean's lingering boom.
O rich remembrancer of worlds unknown
For which I am long homesick, sing once more!

[He draws a chair to the window and sits]

BEATRICE'S Song [further off]
The aloe feds the year of years,
Wakes, and the wandering bees it calls —

[The song ends abruptly, he looks out again]

GUASCONTI

I knew I should see nothing; save the glow
Of noon o'er that dread garden, where methinks
Each venomous thing sprouts rankly as the weeds
Upon forgotten graves. In the deep hush
No cricket's tune is heard, only the stir
Of some quick-darting lizard. Sleeping snakes
Bask on hot stones, coiled furies, in the sun,
Enough to furnish cold Medusa's hair;
And snake-like plants, nameless in mortal tongue.
Pant from their gorgeous flowers, drinking the blaze,
Subtle intoxication. I grow faint
With the sweet horror. O that song! That song
Voluptuous Lilith sang o'er Adam's sleep.
And flushed his blood with sensuous sorcery!

THE PATHFINDER

By G A Greene

Full of world-weariness, and of the sense
Of unachievement, lies the toiler down
Who hath made smooth the way, but sees the crown
Fade in the sunset far through depths immense

Of unassaulted heaven: vain vision, hence!
Yet soon again amid the shadows brown
He striveth on who reacheth not: renown
Was not his aim: he hath his recompense.

Because to aspire is better than to attain:
Because the will is nobler than the deed,
The blossom glorious more than is the fruit;

The worker knows he hath not striven in vain;
They shall arrive with winged and arrowy speed
Who follow far his solitary foot.

THE BROKEN TRYST

By Arthur Symons

That day a fire was in my blood;

I could have sung; joy wrapt me round;
The men I met seemed all so good,
I scarcely knew I trod the ground.

How easy seemed all toil! I laughed
To think that once I hated it.
The sunlight thrilled like wine, I quaffed
Delight divine and infinite.

The very day was not too long;
I felt so patient; I could wait.
Being certain. So, the hours in song
Chimed out the minutes of my fate.

For she was coming, she, at last,
I knew: I knew that bolts and bars
Could stay her not; my heart throbbed fast,
I was not more certain of the stars.

The twilight came, grew deeper; now
The hour struck, minutes passed, and still
The passionate fervour of her vow
Rang in my heart's ear audible.

I had no doubt at all: I knew
That she would come, and I was then
Most certain, while the minutes flew:
Ah, how I scorned all other men!

Next moment! Ah! it was — was not!
I heard the stillness of the street.
Night came. The stars had not forgot.
The moonlight fell about my feet.

So I rebuked my heart, and said:
'Be still, for she is coming, see.
Next moment — coming. Ah, her tread,
I hear it coming — it is she!'

And then a woman passed. The hour
Rang heavily along the air.
I had no hope, I had no power
To think — for thought was but despair.

A thing had happened. What? My brain
Dared not so much as guess the thing.
And yet the sun would rise again
Next morning! I stood marvelling.

NEW WORDS AND OLD

By Edwin J Ellis

I

'In the same day thou eatest thou shalt die.'
Oh long, short day, even now we see appear
Thy sunrise hope, thy chill of evening fear
When the reproving Voice comes wandering by.
Thou hast done well to take eternity
From this false world of ours, but leave it near.
The little door of death is always here;
Thou openest our cage that we may fly.
Some perfect things thou leavest, the white life
Of the heavy lily in the month of June
Thou hast not sullied, nor the wood-bird's tune,
Nor the boy's dream that he shall find for wife
So sweet a maid that even in love's high noon
Pure prayer shall stay his kisses' purer strife.

II

Unfearing, like a new-caught lion wild
Who treads despair and meets the triumphant crowd,
So Adam came, when the voice called aloud.
Then God, his image still but half defiled
Saw darkening in the face of his own child,
Whom wisdom had made modest, but not bow'd,
Who, hating death, forgot not to be proud.
Who sinned from love, and sought no mercy mild.
'Who told thee thou wert naked?' Ah: who told?
'Who told me that this woman at my side.
Whom thou hast given, and made so tender-eyed.
Was less forgiveable to Justice Old
Than unto me, but yesterday untried?'
But Christ has died, and man is no more bold.

III

The Rose and Lily by the golden Gate
Of Heaven's own garden, where the trailing dress
Of the sweet virgin, followed by a press

Of angels among angels fortunate.
Being the guard of her, immaculate,
Had now but passed and left a sacredness
Like perfume in the air that God shall bless, —
The Rose and Lily gently, without hate,
Disputed which should be the flower of choice,
'For being white as I,' the Lily cried,
'Mary was chosen.' Then with tenderer voice,
'But loved for being like me,' the Rose replied.
Returning, Mary laid upon her breast
Both flowers, and none could answer which was best.

IV

So it were strange if I should close my eyes
And fear to find God's mercy on the shore,
Did I this night pass on for evermore
Beyond the level rays of the sunrise.
I come not with a claim for Paradise;
Yet though I shook the Tree of Evil sore,
And though the fruit I tasted to the core,
To go unto the Father I will arise.
Shall He that bade us to forgive, but now,
The trespasser, though trespass brought dismay
And poverty, and pain, e'er He allow
That entrance to forgiveness we might pray, —
Shall God— That is not hurt— still turn away?
I am unworthy. Father, but not Thou.

A RING'S SECRET

By T W Rolleston

Can you forgive me, that I wear,
Dearest, a curl of sunny hair
Not yours, yet for the sake of love
And plighted troth it minds me of?
'Tis in this quaint old signet ring,
A curious, chased engraven thing
I bought because it charm'd my eye
And told of the last century.
Pure gold it was, but dull and blotched.
And brightening it one day I touch'd
A spring that ope'd a little lid,
And there, for generations hid

In its small shrine of pallid gold
— They made such toys in days of old —
A shred of golden hair lay curled;
Worth all the gold of all the world
To some one once, who now — Heigh ho,
That was a hundred years ago!

But dearest, if he loved as I,
He loved unto eternity.

THE WEDDING OF PALE BRONWEN

By Ernest Rhys

I

The wind was waked by the morning light,
And it cried in the gray birch-tree,
And the cry was plain in Bronwen's bower,
'Oh, Bronwen, come to me!'

Pale, pale sleeps Bronwen, pale she wakes,
'What bird to my bower is flown?'
For my lover, Red Ithel, is at the wars
Before Jerusalem town.'

But still the wind sang in the tree,
'Come forth, 'tis your wedding morn.
And you must be wed in Holy Land
Ere your little babe is born.'

And still the wind had her true-love's cry,
'Kind Bronwen, come! ' until
She could not rest, and rose to look
To the sea beyond Morva Hill.

And afar came the cry over Morva Hill,
'Kind Bronwen, come to me! '
Till she could not stay, for very love.
And stole away to the sea.

She crossed the hill to the fishing-boats.
And away she sailed so fine,
'Is it far, my love, in the summer sun
To the shores of fair Palestine?'

There was no sun at sea that day.
To watch pale Bronwen drown.
But the sun was hot on the deadly sands
Before Jerusalem town.

All day Red Ithel lay dying there.
But he thought of the far-off sea;
And he cried all day till his lips grew white,
'Kind Bronwen, come to me!'

And so it passed till the evening time,
And then the sea-wind came.
And he thought he lay on Morva Hill
And heard her call his name.

He heard her voice, he held her hand,
'This is the day,' she said.
'And this is the hour that Holy Church
Has given for us to wed.'

There was no strength in him to speak,
But his eyes had yet their say,
'Kind Bronwen, now we will be wed
Forever and ever and aye!'

III

Beneath the sea pale Bronwen lies,
Red Ithel beneath the sand;
But they are one in Holy Church,
One in love's Holy Land.

Red Ithel lies by Jerusalem town,
And she in the deep sea lies;
But I trow their little babe was born
In the gardens of Paradise.

BEAUTY ACCURST

By Richard Le Gallienne

I am so fair that wheresoe'er I wend

Men yearn with strange desire to kiss my face,
Stretch out their hands to touch me as I pass,
And women follow me from place to place.

A poet writing honey of his dear
Leaves the wet page, — ah, leaves it long to dry.
The bride forgets it is her marriage morn.
The bridegroom too forgets as I go by.

Within the street where my strange feet shall stray
All markets hush and traffickers forget.
In my gold head forget their meaner gold,
The poor man grows unmindful of his debt.

Two lovers kissing in a secret place,
Should I draw nigh, will never kiss again;
I come between the king and his desire.
And where I am all loving else is vain.

Lo! as I walk along the woodland way
Strange creatures leer at me with uncouth love,
And from the grass reach upward to my breast,
And to my mouth lean from the boughs above.

The sleepy kine move round me in desire
And press their oozy lips upon my hair,
Toads kiss my feet and creatures of the mire,
The snails will leave their shells to watch me there

But all this worship — what is it to me?
I smite the ox and crush the toad in death,
I only know I am so very fair
And that the world was made to give me breath.

I only wait the hour when God shall rise
Up from the star where he so long hath sat,
And bow before the wonder of my eyes.
And set ins there — I am so fair as that.

O MORS! QUAM AMARA EST MEMORIA TUA HOMINI PACEM HABENTI IN SUBSTANTIIS SUIS!

By Ernest Dowson

Exceeding sorrow
Consumeth my sad heart!
Because to-morrow,

We must depart,
Now is exceeding sorrow
All my part!

Give over playing:
Cast thy viol away:
Merely laying
Thy head my way:
Prithee! give over playing,
Grave or gay.

Be no word spoken:
Weep nothing; let a pale
Silence, unbroken
Silence prevail:
Prithee! be no word spoken,
Lest I fail.

Forget to-morrow,
Weep nothing: merely lay,
For silent sorrow,
Thine head my way;
Let us forget to-morrow,
This last day!

THE SONNET

By G A Greene

I hear the quatrains' rolling melody,
The second answering back her sister's sounds
Like a repeated music, that resounds
A second time with varying harmony:

Then come the tercets with full-voiced reply.
And close the solemn strain in sacred bounds,
While all the time one growing thought expounds
One palpitating passion's ecstasy.

Ah! could I hear thy thoughts so answer mine
As quatrain echoes quatrain, soft and low.
Two hearts in rhyme and time one golden glow;

If so two lives one music might entwine,
What melody of life were mine and thine.
Till song-like comes the ending all must know!

A BURDEN OF EASTER VIGIL

By Lionel Johnson

A while meet Doubt and Faith:
For either sigheth, and saith;
That He is dead
To-day: the linen cloths cover His head,
That hath at last, whereon to rest; a rocky bed.

Come! for the pangs are done,
That overcast the sun,
So bright to-day!
And moved the Roman soldier: come away!
Hath sorrow more to weep? hath pity more to say?

Why wilt thou linger yet?
Think on dark Olivet;
On Calvary Stem:
Think, from the happy birth at Bethlehem,
To this last woe and passion at Jerusalem!

This only can be said:
He loved us all; is dead;
May rise again.
But if He rise not? Over the far main,
The sun of glory falls indeed: the stars are plain.

TO ONE BELOVED

By John Todhunter

Away from thee, my love! Away from thee?
O, in the soul of sense, never more near,
Thy love broods in the genial glow of day,
Thy tender solace fills the hush of night!

All hopes or fears, all triumph or defeat,
All shy vicissitudes the spirit knows,
Seem but the changes of that shadowy clime
Where Love doth bless thee from the spells of change.

All moving tales, all beauty, all delight.

Earth's multitudinous music or the sea's,
All sweet and shuddering chords from Life's rich lute
Set my lone pulses murmuring unto thee:

Murmuring in murmurs, neither passionate words,
Nor music wafting them on wings of might,
Nor seraph silence with her golden tongue.
Can ever all remurmur to thy heart.

MUSIC AND MEMORY

(To K W)

By Arthur Symons

Across the tides of music, in the night,
Her magical face,
A light upon it as the happy light
Of dreams in some delicious place
Under the moonlight in the night.

Music, soft throbbing music in the night,
Her memory swims
Into the brain, a carol of delight;
The cup of music overbrims
With wine of memory, in the night.

Her face across the music, in the night.
Her face a refrain,
A light that sings along the waves of light,
A memory that returns again,
Music in music, in the night.

IN A NORMAN CHURCH

By Victor Plarr

As over incense-laden air
Stole winter twilight, soft and dim,
The folk arose from their last prayer —
When hark! the children's hymn.

Round yon great pillar, circlewise.
The singers stand up two and two —

Small lint-haired girls from whose young eyes
The gray sea looks at you.

Now heavenward the pure music wins
With cadence soft and silvery beat.
In flutes and subtle violins
Are harmonies less sweet.

It is a chant with plaintive ring.
And rhymes and refrains old and quaint.
Oh Monseigneur Saint Jacques,' they sing,
And 'Oh Assisi's Saint.'

Through deepening dusk one just can see
The little white-capped heads that move
In time to lines turned rhythmically
And starred with names of love.

Bred in no gentle silken ease,
Trained to expect no splendid fate,
They are but peasant children these,
Of very mean estate.

Nay, is that true? To-night perhaps
Un worldlier eyes had well discerned
Among those little gleaming caps
An aureole that burned.

For once 'twas thought the Gates of Pearl
Best opened to the poor that trod
The path of the meek peasant girl
Who bore the Son of God.

FATHER GILLIGAN

(A legend told by the people of Castleisland, Kerry)

By W B Yeats

The old priest Peter Gilligan
Was weary night and day,
For half his flock were in their beds
Or under green sods lay.

Once while he nodded on a chair,
At the moth-hour of eve,

Another poor man sent for him.
And he began to grieve.

'I have no rest, nor joy, nor peace,
For people die and die;'
And after cried he, 'God forgive!
My body spake, not I!'

And then, half-lying on the chair,
He knelt, prayed, fell asleep;
And the moth-hour went from the fields,
And stars began to peep.

They slowly into millions grew,
And leaves shook in the wind;
And God covered the world with shade,
And whispered to mankind.

Upon the time of sparrow chirp,
When the moths came once more,
The old priest Peter Gilligan
Stood upright on the floor.

'Ochone, ochone! the man has died.
While I slept on the chair';
He roused his horse out of its sleep.
And rode with little care.

He rode now as he never rode.
By rocky lane and fen;
The sick man's wife opened the door:
'Father! you come again!'

'And is the poor man dead?' he cried.
'He died an hour ago.'
The old priest Peter Gilligan
In grief swayed to and fro.

'When you were gone he turned and died,
As merry as a bird.'
The old priest Peter Gilligan
He knelt him at that word.

'He who hath made the night of stars
For souls who tire and bleed
Sent one of His great angels down
To help me in my need.

'He who is wrapped in purple robes,
With planets in his care,
Had pity on the least of things
Asleep upon a chair,'

AMOR UMBRATILIS

By Ernest Dowson

A gift of silence, Sweet!
Who may not ever hear:
To lay down at your unobservant feet,
Is all the gift I bear.

I have no songs to sing,
That you should heed or know:
I have no lilies, in full hands, to fling,
Across the path you go.

I cast my flowers away,
Blossoms unmeet for you:
The garland, I have gathered, in my day;
My rose-mary and rue.

I watch you pass and pass,
Serene and cold: I lay
My lips upon your trodden, daisied grass,
And turn my life away.

Yea, for I cast you, Sweet!
This one gift, you shall take:
Like ointment, on your unobservant feet.
My silence, for your sake.

AT THE HEARTH

By Edwin J Ellis

The kettle sang beside the bars
A tender ballad soft and low;
Time came down from the far-off stars
And warmed his feet before the glow.

Then Love drew near the further side, —

Between the two, my bride and I, —
And silent I, and still my bride,
And Love, lest Time should rouse and fly.

We might have lingered there till doom,
If doom could come with Time asleep;
But Pity crept into the room.
Saying, oh Time, thy children weep.

Then Time rose up and took his scythe;
The frightened kettle ceased to sing;
But Pity, through her tears, grew blythe,
And led him forth and kissed his wing.

KEATS' GRAVE

(Written when it was proposed to make a high-road over it)

By G A Greene

Dust unto dust? Ye are the dust of Time,
Immortals, whose mortality is o'er;
Names writ in water once — now evermore
Carved on remembering hearts in gold of rhyme.

What though above your heads the pantomime
Of vulgar traffic clash with daily roar?
'Tis the same load in life your spirits bore,
The world's indifference to souls sublime.

So all mankind moves on with ceaseless tread,
Tho' the far goal yon mystic shadow bars,
Along a road whose dust is heroes' lives.

Sacred no less the soil, than overhead
That highway to whose end no sight arrives,
A riven road ablaze with dust of stars.

ON MARLOWE*

By Ernest Rhys

With wine and blood and reckless harlotry
He sped the heroic flame of English verse;

Bethink ye, Rhymers, what your claim may be,
Who in smug suburbs put the Muse to nurse?

The Rhymers held a 'Marlowe' night, and the writer having brought no rhyme of celebration, was punished by a command to produce one on the spot, in the writing which he took a friendly revenge!

AT CITOYENNE TUSSAUD'S

By Victor Plarr

The place is full of whispers — 'Mark you, sirs,
This one is he who struck our moralists mute
Before the crime which proved him wholly brute!
Mark well his face!' The gaping sight-seers
Nudge one another, and no tongue but stirs
In awe-struck comment on hat, coat and boot
Mean smirking smile, base air of smug repute,
Worn by some prince of viler murderers!

Nay, I like most these lank-tressed doctrinaires
Who cluster round their powerless guillotine.
Aquiline, delicate, dark, their thin cheeks mired
By their own blood — these Carriers and Heberts.
They only look so proud and so serene:
They only look so infinitely tired!

BALLADE OF THE 'CHESHIRE CHEESE' IN FLEET STREET

By T W Rolleston

I know a home of antique ease
Within the smoky city's pale,
A spot wherein the spirit sees
Old London through a thinner veil.
The modern world, so stiff and stale,
You leave behind you, when you please.
For long clay pipes and great old ale
And beefsteaks in the 'Cheshire Cheese.'

Beneath this board Burke's, Goldsmith's knees
Were often thrust — so runs the tale —
'Twas here the Doctor took his ease,
And wielded speech that, like a flail,
Threshed out the golden truth: All hail

Great souls! that met on nights like these,
Till morning made the candles pale,
And revellers left the 'Cheshire Cheese.'

By kindly sense, and old decrees
Of England's use, they set their sail—
We press to never-furrowed seas,
For vision-worlds we breast the gale,
And still we seek and still we fail,
For still the 'glorious phantom' flees —
Ah, well! no phantom are the ale
And beefsteaks of the ' Cheshire Cheese.'

Envoi

If doubts or debts thy soul assail,
If Fashion's forms its current freeze.
Try a long pipe, a glass of ale,
And supper in the 'Cheshire Cheese.'

THE LAST MUSIC

By Lionel Johnson

Calmly, breathe calmly all your music, maids!
Breathe a calm music over my dead queen.
All your lives long, you have nor heard, nor seen,
Fairer than she, whose hair in sombre braids
With beauty overshades
Her brow broad and serene.

Surely she hath lain so an hundred years:
Peace is upon her, old as the world's heart.
Breathe gently, music! Music done, depart:
And leave me in her presence to my tears,
With music in mine ears;
For sorrow hath its art.

Music, more music, sad and slow! She lies
Dead: and more beautiful than early morn.
Discrowned am I, and of her looks forlorn:
Alone vain memories immortalize
The way of her soft eyes.
Her virginal voice low-borne.

The balm of gracious death now laps her round,

As once life gave her grace beyond her peers.
Strange! that I loved this lady of the spheres,
To sleep by her at last in common ground:
When kindly death hath bound
Mine eyes, and sealed mine ears.

Maidens! make a low music: merely make
Silence a melody, no more. This day,
She travels down a pale and lonely way:
Now for a gentle comfort, let her take
Such music, for her sake,
As mourning love can play.

Holy my queen lies in the arms of death:
Music moves over her still face, and I
Lean breathing love over her. She will lie
In earth thus calmly, under the wind's breath:
The twilight wind that saith:
Rest! worthy found ^ to die.

A DEATH IN THE FOREST

By Arthur Symons

The wind is loud among the trees to-night,
It sweeps the heavens where the stars are white.
I know: it is the angel with the sword.
Ah, not the woman, not the woman, Lord!

The wind is loud, I hear it in my brain,
I hear the rushing voices of the rain.
Hers in the rain, and his that once implored.
Ah, not the woman, not the woman, Lord!

Hands in the trees, hands in the flowing grass,
They wave to catch my spirit as I pass.
I have no hope to pass the ghastly ford.
Ah, not the woman, not the woman, Lord!

I see her tresses floating down the wind:
Her eyes are bright: it is for these I sinned.
We sinned, and I have had my own reward.
Ah, not the woman, not the woman. Lord!

She has a little mouth, a little chin:
God made her to be beautiful in sin,

God made her perfectly, to be adored.
Ah, not the woman, not the woman. Lord!

We sinned, but it is I who pay the price:
I say that she shall dwell in Paradise.
For me the feast in hell is on the board.
Ah, not the woman, not the woman, Lord!

'ONLI DEATHE'

(Inscribed in an Old Ring)

By Ernest Radford

'Only death us twain shall sever:'
'Nay, that he shall not do,' she saith:
'The Love I give you is for Ever:
Dark Death for all his dire endeavour
Decrees no parting — only death.'

AD DOMNULAM SUAM

By Ernest Dowson

Little lady of my heart!
Just a little longer,
Love me: we will pass and part,
Ere this love grow stronger.

I have loved thee, Child! too well,
To do aught but leave thee:
Nay! my lips should never tell
Any tale, to grieve thee.

Little lady of my heart!
Just a little longer,
I may love thee: we will part.
Ere my love grow stronger.

Soon thou leavest fairy-land;
Darker grow thy tresses:
Soon no more of hand in hand;
Soon no more caresses!

Little lady of my heart!
Just a little longer,
Be a child: then, we will part,
Ere this love grow stronger.

DEDICATION OF 'IRISH TALES'

By W B Yeats

There was a green branch hung with many a bell
When her own people ruled in wave-worn Eri,
And from its murmuring greenness, calm of faery
— A Druid kindness — on all hearers fell.

It charmed away the merchant from his guile,
And turned the farmer's memory from his cattle.
And hushed in sleep the roaring ranks of battle,
For all who heard it dreamed a little while.

Ah, Exiles wandering over many seas,
Spinning at all times Eri's good to-morrow.
Ah, world-wide Nation, always growing Sorrow,
I also bear a bell branch full of ease.

I tore it from green boughs winds tossed and hurled.
Green boughs of tossing always, weary, weary,
I tore it from the green boughs of old Eri,
The willow of the many-sorrowed world.

Ah, Exiles, wandering over many lands,
My bell branch murmurs: the gay bells bring laughter,
Leaping to shake a cobweb from the rafter;
The sad bells bow the forehead on the hands.

A honied ringing, under the new skies
They bring you memories of old village faces.
Cabins gone now, old well-sides, old dear places.
And men who loved the cause that never dies.

QUATRAIN

THE EPITAPH ON HAFIZ, A YOUNG LINNET

By Ernest Rhys

Dead here lies Hafiz, might have lived so long,
And turned his morning worm to morning song:
Now worms be glad, on Hafiz whet your teeth,
Until poor Hafiz' sexton lie beneath.

JAVANESE DANCERS: A SILHOUETTE

By Arthur Symons

Twitched strings, the clang of metal, beaten drums,
Dull, shrill, continuous, disquieting;
And now the stealthy dancer comes
Undulantly with cat-like steps that cling;

Smiling between her painted lids a smile
Motionless, unintelligible, she twines
Her fingers into mazy lines,
Twining her scarves across them all the while.

One, two, three, four, step forth, and, to and fro,
Delicately and imperceptibly.
Now swaying gently in a row,
Now interthreading slow and rhythmically,

Still with fixed eyes, monotonously still.
Mysteriously, with smiles inanimate.
With lingering feet that undulate.
With sinuous fingers, spectral hands that thrill,

The little amber-coloured dancers move,
Like little painted figures on a screen,
Or phantom dancers haply seen
Among the shadows of a magic grove.

CHORUS

(From Iphigeneia in Aulis)*

By John Todhunter

Strophe
Where shall we find, in what remote
And dark abyss of time, the dread beginning

Of mortal woe: the crescent plague that smote
The germ of the world, the sin that set men sinning?
Or shall we blame for the evils of our state
Man's fatal fault, or faultful fate?
And why, and whence, and how begotten, came
That flying Mischief to the banquet-house,
Where the Olympians in divine carouse
Pledged Peleus and the silver-footed dame;
Till, shining there, the sudden fruit
Made spite in heaven: whence the contending Three
Naked in Ida; the bribed shepherd's flute
Cast by, and insolent rape launched on the sea.
And Helen and these wars; whence Peleus' son
Foredoomed, and no rest from calamity;
But woes in tireless tribe still raging on,
New sins, and innocent deaths?

Antistrophe

O, might we hear that song ye heard,
Ye pines, ye laurels, and thick-flowering myrtles,
On Pelion's flank, what time your leaves were stirr'd
With tuneful breath, when in their sacred kirtles
The Muses came over the mountain-side
To feast with Peleus and his bride!
For surely then they sang, the bright-haired Nine,
To the majestic tripping of their feet,
A nine-fold paean, solemn, strange and sweet,
Of the ancient gods, and mysteries divine:
Fate and freewill, the hidden laws
That bind man's life; why good was doomed to be
Twin-born with evil; wherefore without pause
They strive; yet from their strife the harmony
That wakes new stars in heaven; yet, for our needs,
Heroes, and hearts that mould eternity.
And hopes that conquer fate, and noble deeds.
Virtues, and valorous deaths.

Epode

But, O ye Muses, who, since Time began
Most loved in heaven, most loving man.
Have talked with hoary Wisdom from your birth,
Sing to our inward ear, O sing again
That sage and solemn strain.
Make musical the riddle of the earth!
Make us to hear your ordered lyres
Ringing through chaos, wakening there
That world whereto, through vain desires
And woes, and strife, and much despair,

And many sins, the world aspires!

Not a translation from Euripides.

TO A GREEK GEM

By Victor Plarr

Was it the signet of an Antonine —
This middle-finger ring, whose bezel glows
With the most lovely of intaglios
E'er wrought by craftsman in an age divine?
Or was it borne by grim Tiberius' line
At lustful festals and fierce wild beast shows?
Signed it wise edicts, or when Lucan chose
His artful liberal death was it the sign?

I cannot tell, nor can this lucent toy.
I only know that these small graven forms.
This cymbal-playing maenad and this boy,
In their delightful beauty shall live on,
Crannied 'mong crashing rocks, when Time's last storms
Have whelmed us in the sands we build upon.

ARTS LOUGH

Glenmalure, Co. Wicklow

By G A Greene

Lone lake half lost amidst encircling hills,
Beneath the imprisoning mountain-crags concealed;
Who liest to the wide earth unrevealed;
To whose repose the brief and timorous rills

Bring scarce a murmur: — thou whose sight instils
Despair; o'er whom his dark disdainful shield
Abrupt Clogherna 'gainst the sun doth wield,
And thy dim face with deepening shadow fills:

O poet soul! companionless and sad,
Tho' half the daytime long a death-like shade
Athwart thy depths with constant horror lies.

Thou art not ever in dejection clad,
But showest still, as in a glass displayed,
The limitless unfathomable skies.

IN FALMOUTH HARBOUR

By Lionel Johnson

The large, calm harbour lies below
Long, terraced lines of circling light:
Without, the deep sea currents flow:
And here are stars, and night.

No sight, no sound, no living stir,
But such as perfect the still bay:
So hushed it is, the voyager
Shrinks at the thought of day.

We glide by many a lanterned mast;
Our mournful horns blow wild to warn
Yon looming pier: the sailors cast
Their ropes, and watch for morn.

Strange murmurs from the sleeping town,
And sudden creak of lonely oars
Crossing the water, travel down
The roadstead, the dim shores.

A charm is on the silent bay;
Charms of the sea, charms of the land.
Memories of open wind convey
Peace to this harbour strand.

Far off, Saint David's crags descend
On seas of desolate storm: and far
From this pure rest, the Land's drear End,
And ruining waters, are.

Well was it worth to have each hour
Of high and perilous blowing wind:
For here, for now, deep peace hath power
To conquer the worn mind.

I have passed over the rough sea,
As over the white harbour bar:
And this Death's dreamland is to me,

Led hither by a star.

And what shall dawn be? Hush thee, nay!
Soft, soft is night, and calm, and still:
Save that day cometh, what of day
Knowest thou: good, or ill?

Content thee! Not the annulling light
Of any pitiless dawn is here;
Thou art alone with ancient night:
And all the stars are clear.

Only the night air, and the dream;
Only the far, sweet smelling wave;
The stilly sounds, the circling gleam,
Are thine: and thine the grave.

A CHOICE OF LIKENESSES

By Ernest Radford

'Nay,' said the husband, 'give him this,'
In manifest alarm,
'This is her very likeness; — that
Has but a sudden charm.'

'The look that flashes into light
And quickly dies away
May blind some passer: as for me,
I love the looks that stay.'

And I but said: (what could I say —
Not dreaming any harm?)
'They're yours, old friend, her looks that stay.
Spare then to me — she surely may —
This glance of sudden charm.'

TO AUTUMN

By Richard Le Gallienne

The year grows still again, the surging wake
Of full-sailed summer folds its furrows up,
As after passing of an argosy

Old silence settles back upon the sea,
And ocean grows as placid as a cup.
Spring the young, morn, and Summer the strong noon,
Have dreamed and done and died for Autumn's sake;
Autumn that finds not for a loss so dear
Solace in stack and garner hers too soon —
Autumn, the faithful widow of the year.

Autumn, a poet once so full of song,
Wise in all rhymes of blossom and of bud,
Hath lost the early magic of his tongue.
And hath no passion in his failing blood.
Hear ye no sound of sobbing in the air?
'Tis his, — low bending in a secret lane,
Late blooms of second childhood in his hair,
He tries old magic like a dotard mage;
Tries spell and spell to weep and try again:
Yet not a daisy hears, and everywhere
The hedgerow rattles like an empty cage.

He hath no pleasure in his silken skies,
Nor delicate ardours of the yellow land;
Yea! dead, for all its gold, the woodland lies,
And all the throats of music filled with sand.
Neither to him across the stubble field
May stack or garner any comfort bring,
Who loveth more this jasmine he hath made,
The little tender rhyme he yet can sing.
Than yesterday with all its pompous yield
Or all its shaken laurels on his head.

VANITAS

By Ernest Dowson

Beyond the need of weeping,
Beyond the reach of hands,
May she be quietly sleeping.
In what dim nebulous lands?
Ah, she who understands!

The long, long winter weather.
These many years and days,
Since she, and Death, together.
Left me the wearier ways:
And now, these tardy bays!

The crown and victor's token:
How are they worth to-day?
The one word left unspoken.
It were late now to say:
But cast the palm away!

For once, ah once, to meet her,
Drop laurel from tired hands;
Her cypress were the sweeter,
In her oblivious lands:
Haply she understands!

Yet, crossed that weary river,
In some ulterior land,
Or anywhere, or ever,
Will she stretch out a hand?
And will she understand?

A FAIRY SONG

Sung by 'the Good People' over the outlaw Michael Buyer and his bride, who had escaped into the mountains

By W B Yeats

We who are old, old and gay,
O so old.
Thousands of years, thousands of years.
If all were told:

Give to these children new from the world
Silence and love,
And the long dew-dropping hours of the night
And the stars above:

Give to these children new from the world
Rest far from men.
Is anything better, anything better?
Tell it us then:

Us who are old, old and gay,
O so old.
Thousands of years, thousands of years,
If all were told.

MOTHERS OF MEN

By Edwin J Ellis

When fire and life are apart and twain,
And anger sleeps, and her sister pain,
And softly doses, —
His eyelid closes, —
The tired young love, and his wing reposes.

Then gather, like shades of the Earth's first mood
In a sweet and compassionate multitude,'
Oh you who are old,
And whose eyes have told
The young wide eyes that their first light hold, —

Have loved, and have told of the long life-change, —
Why night is faithful, and daylight strange, —
How the dark increase
Of the seed called peace
Is the flower of hope, and the fruit release.

Come one, who art near me, and all set free,
Come forth from the earth, or the dull gray sea,
Come now, for a grace
In your light finds place
That weight cannot cover, nor dreams efface.

Come near, I would bend to you, mother of men,
Whose calm soft answering face again
Gives fear and joy
As when loves employ
The lips of the girl and the young-lipped boy.

Come near, for all mothers are near in you.
Make holy the lips and the eyes renew
That in youth have wandered
And favour squandered
In kisses unweighed and in tears unpondered.

Oh not by the morning, so sweet as now
In the maid-like droop of a bird-filled bough.
From the bough wind-stirred
Is a music heard.
Nor more shall the tree love the small brown bird.

Nor blue of the noon as revered, nor red
So loved in the wine of the sun, wide-spread,
Nor a child that laughed.
Nor a lightning shaft
More white, nor freer the white-sailed craft.

For you, oh mothers of men, are more
When the kiss bids open, and hearts outpour.
Than all of these,
Nor on lands nor seas
Shall love without your love bring me ease.

CHATTERTON IN HOLBORN

By Ernest Rhys

From country fields I came, that hid
The harvest mice at play,
And followed care, whose calling bid
To London's troubled way.

And there I wandered, far and wide
And came, ere day was done,
Where Holborn poured its civic tide
Beneath the autumn sun.

So hot the sun, so great the throng,
I gladly stayed my feet
To hear a captive linnet's song
Accuse the London street.

Above, an ancient roof-tree bowed
Its gabled head, and made
Obeisance to the modern crowd
That swept athwart its shade.

Below, an open window kept
Old books in grave array,
Where critics drowsed, and poets slept,
Till Grub Street's judgment day.

One book I drew forth carelessly —
The book of Rowley's rhyme,
That Chatterton, in seigneury
Of song, bore out of time.

The merchant of such ware unseen,
Watched spider-like the street,
He came forth, gray and spider-thin,
And talked with grave conceit.

Old books, old times — he drew them nigh,
At Chatterton's pale spell:
"Twas Brook Street yonder saw him die.
Old Holborn knew him well.'

The words brought back in sudden sway
That tale of poet's doom.
It seemed the boy but yesterday
Died in his lonely room.

Without the press of men was heard,
I heard, as one who dreamed,
The hurrying throng, the singing bird.
And yesterday it seemed.

And as I turned to go, the tale
This pensive requiem made,
As though within the graveyard rail,
The boy was newly laid.

Requiem

Perhaps, who knows, the hurrying throng
Had hopeless signs for him;
I fancy how he wandered long
Until the light grew dim.

The windows saw him come and pass.
And come and go again;
And still the throng swept by — alas!
The barren face of men.

And when the day was gone, the way
Led down to the lethal deeps:
Sweet Life, what requiem to say?
'Tis well, 'tis well, he sleeps.

TO A PASSIONIST

By Lionel Johnson

Clad in a vestment wrought with passion flowers;
Celebrant of one Passion; called by name
Passionist: is thy world, one world with ours?
Thine, a like heart? Thy very soul, the same?

Thou pleadest an eternal sorrow: we
Praise the still changing beauty of this earth.
Passionate good and evil, thou dost see:
Our eyes behold the dreams of death and birth.

We love the joys of men: we love the dawn.
Red with the sun, and with the pure dew pearled.
Thy stern soul feels, after the sun withdrawn,
How much pain goes to perfecting the world.

Canst thou be right? Is thine the very truth?
Stands then our life in so forlorn a state?
Nay, but thou wrongest us; thou wrong'st our youth;
Who dost our happiness compassionate.

And yet! and yet! O royal Calvary!
Whence divine sorrow triumphed through years past!
Could ages bow before mere memory?
Those passion flowers must blossom, to the last.

Purple they bloom, the splendour of a King:
Crimson they bleed, the sacrament of Death:
About our thrones and pleasaunces they cling.
Where guilty eyes read, what each blossom saith.

FREEDOM IN A SUBURB

By Ernest Radford

He leaned upon the narrow wall
That set the limit to his ground,
And marvelled, thinking of it all,
That he such happiness had found.

There long he sat in perfect peace:
He smoked his pipe, he thanked his stars;
(His stars — unnumbered in the Lease);
He blest the subterranean cars

That bore him back the home to win
Where in the morn he'd left a heart

Not trusted in the devil's din
Of London's damned money mart.

QUATRAIN

LES BOURGEOISES

By Ernest Rhys

Their health they to their horses give:
They, dully blinking, ride behind,
And yawn again, who do not live,
But seek for life and never find.

DRIFTING

By G A Greene

As one that drifting in an open boat
Down a broad river, singing, wayfareth,
While on the banks few listeners hear the note,

And pause and hearken, till the lapsing stream
Seaward bears on the bark whence murmureth
Music that fails and dies, a flying dream:

Such is my song. Borne downward on the tide,
I cannot tell what echoes of my breath
Are caught by listeners on the riverside:
I and my songs glide onward unto death.

VILLANELLE OF SUNSET

By Ernest Dowson

Come hither, child! and rest:
        This is the end of day,
Behold the weary West!
Sleep rounds with equal zest
        Man's toil and children's play:
Come hither, child! and rest.
My white bird, seek thy nest.

Thy drooping head down lay:
Behold the weary West!
Now are the flowers confest
        Of slumber: sleep, as they!
Come hither, child! and rest.
Now eve is manifest.
        And homeward lies our way:
Behold the weary West!
Tired flower! upon my breast,
        I would wear thee, alway:
Come hither, child! and rest;
Behold, the weary West!

THE LAKE ISLE OF INNLSFREE

By W B Yeats

I will arise and go now, and go to Innisfree,
And a small cabin build there, of clay and wattles made;
Nine bean rows will I have there, a hive for the honey bee,
And live alone in the bee- loud glade.

And I shall have some peace there, for peace comes dropping slow,
Dropping from the veils of the morning to where the cricket sings;
There midnight's all a glimmer, and noon a purple glow,
And evening full of the linnet's wings.

I will arise and go now, for always night and day
I hear lake water lapping with low sounds on the shore;
While I stand on the roadway or on the pavements gray,
I hear it in the deep heart's core.

A SUNDIAL— FLOWERS OF TLME

(In memory of R A L, Sculptor)

By Ernest Radford

Mark how with loving hand he wrought
Here on the dial that counts the hours
Thy sad great figure; winged Time
Set heavy-hearted mid the flowers.

Ah, even whilst he wrought did he

Close a great bargain with the years,
The sooner with these flowers to be
That for their nurture have thy tears.

TWILIGHT-PIECE

By Victor Plarr

The golden river-reach afar
Kisses the golden skies of even,
And there's the first faint lover's star
Alight along the walls of heaven.

The river murmurs to the boughs,
The boughs make music each to each.
And still an amorous west wind soughs
And loiters down the lonesome reach.

And here on the slim arch that spans
The rippling stream, in dark outline,
You see the poor old fisherman's
Bowed form and patient rod and line.

A picture better than all art.
Since none could catch that sunset stain.
Or set in the soft twilight's heart
This small strange touch of human pain!

SUNSET IN THE CITY

By Richard Le Gallienne

Above the town a monstrous wheel is turning,
With glowing spokes of red,
Low in the west its fiery axle burning;
And, lost amid the spaces overhead,
A vague white moth, the moon, is fluttering.

Above the town an azure sea is flowing
'Mid long peninsulas of shining sand,
From opal unto pearl the moon is growing,
Dropped like a shell upon the changing strand.

Within the town the streets grow strange and haunted,

And, dark against the western lakes of green,
The buildings change to temples, and unwonted
Shadows and sounds creep in where day has been.

Within the town the lamps of sin are flaring.
Poor foolish men that know not what ye are!
Tired traffic still upon his feet is faring —
Two lovers meet and kiss, and watch a star.

AN EPITAPH

By W B Yeats

I dreamed that One had died in a strange place
Near no accustomed hand,
And they had nailed the boards above her face,
The peasants of that land,
And wondering, planted by her solitude
A cypress and a yew.
I came and wrote upon a cross of wood
— Man had no more to do —
'She was more beautiful than thy first love
This lady by the trees,'
And gazed upon the mournful stars above
And heard the mournful breeze.

PROVERBS

By Edwin J Ellis

Comfort for the falling powers;
Sorrow for the prime:
Breathing will for youthful hours;
Later, written rhyme; —

Youth, a furious pondering,
Hardly pardoning breath:
Age a sleep, with wandering;
Dreams, the door of death.

Youth a wakening: life a cry:
Age a sleep: — oh, age a sleep!
Silent loves eternally
His midnight watches keep.

Silent loves and silent stars,
And he their silent guest,
While youth and rhyme, and pain and prime
Serve his eternal rest.

PLATO IN LONDON

By Lionel Johnson

The pure flame of one taper fall
Over the old and comely page:
No harsher light disturb at all
This converse with a treasured sage.
Seemly, and fair, and of the best,
If Plato be our guest,
Should things befall.

Without, a world of noise and cold:
Here, the soft burning of the fire.
And Plato walks, where heavens unfold,
About the home of his desire.
From his own city of high things,
He shows to us, and brings,
Truth of fine gold.

The hours pass; and the fire burns low;
The clear flame dwindles into death:
Shut then the book with care; and so,
Take leave of Plato, with hushed breath,
A little, by the falling gleams.
Tarry the gracious dreams:
And they too go.

Lean from the window to the air:
Hear London's voice upon the night!
Thou hast held converse with things rare:
Look now upon another sight!
The calm stars, in their living skies:
And then, those surging cries,
This restless glare!

That starry music, starry fire.
High above all our noise and glare:
The image of our long desire.
The beauty, and the strength, are there.

And Plato's thought lives, true and clear,
In as august a sphere:
Perchance, far higher.

SONG OF THE SONGSMITHS

(First Anniversary of the Rhymers' Club)

By G A Greene

Here do we meet again.
After a full year's time:
Here do we meet again,
Meet with our old refrain,
Praise of the regal rhyme.
Songsmiths like them who of old
Fashioned their speech of gold
In a far, forgotten clime,
We at that ancient fire
With our young bright breath suspire.
And hammer the golden rhyme,
Hammer the ringing rhyme
Till the echoes tire.

Who is it jeers at our song?
Scoffs at an art sublime?
Who is it jeers at our song?
We who know right from wrong
Worship the godlike rhyme.

Still oil the world-wide breeze,
Over the surge of the seas,
Comes like an echoed chime
The voice of all passions that play
In the dim heart of man always,
With the rush of a rolling rhyme,
The lilt of a lulling rhyme,
To the end of day.

Ours is the prentice-hand;
Yet 'tis in us no crime,
Here in the misty land,
To seek for the fire that was fanned
By kings of the kingly rhyme.
They have gone down to the shade,
Leaving the songs they made

A wreath for the brows of Time,
Still is the great world young;
Not yet is the lyre unstrung,
As it shakes to the quivering rhyme,
Sighs for the resonant rhyme
Of the songs unsung.

Ours are the echoes at least
That fell from that golden prime;
Ours are the echoes at least
Ours are the crumbs from the feast
At the feet of the queenly rhyme:
Ours he the task to prolong
The joy and the sorrow of song
In the mist of years that begrime;
In the clinging mist of the years.,
With reverent toil and with tears,
To hammer the golden rhyme,
Hammer the ringing rhyme
Till the mad world hears.

www.ingramcontent.com/pod-product-compliance
Lightning Source LLC
Chambersburg PA
CBHW021945040426
42448CB00008B/1240